D0118231

Colors of
KENYA

by Fran Sammis
illustrations by Jeni Reeves

COLORS OF THE WORLD

To Sarah—
Enjoy the colors!
Jeni Reeves
2/24/05

Carolrhoda Books, Inc. / Minneapolis

For Dad—with love and thanks for the encouragement, support, and "writer's genes"—F.S.

These illustrations are dedicated to my husband, Dr. S.G. Reeves, who explored the colors of Kenya with me—J.R.

Special thanks to Ben Pike, Professor of African Languages and Literature at the University of MN, for his help. The author wishes to thank Samuel Kiema and Sally Allen for their assistance in the preparation of this book.

Text copyright © 1998 by Fran Sammis
Illustrations copyright © 1998 by Jeni Reeves
Map on page 3 by John Erste

This book is available in two editions:
Library binding by Carolrhoda Books, Inc.
Soft cover by First Avenue Editions
c/o The Lerner Publishing Group
241 First Avenue North
Minneapolis, MN 55401 U.S.A.
Website address: www.lernerbooks.com

Library of Congress Cataloging-in-Publication Data

Sammis, Fran.
  Colors of Kenya / by Fran Sammis ; illustrations by Jeni Reeves ;
 [map on page 3 by John Erste].
    p.   cm. — (Colors of the world)
  Text in English; color terms in English and Swahili.
  Includes index.
  Summary: Explores the different colors found in Kenya's
history, culture, and landscape.
  ISBN 1-57505-280-6 (alk. paper)
  ISBN 1-57505-282-2 (pbk.)
  1. Kenya—Juvenile literature. 2. Colors—Juvenile literature.
[1. Kenya. 2. Color.] I. Reeves, Jeni, ill. II. Title. III. Series.
DT433.522.S26   1998
967.62—dc21   97-35266

Manufactured in the United States of America
1 2 3 4 5 6 – SP – 03 02 01 00 99 98

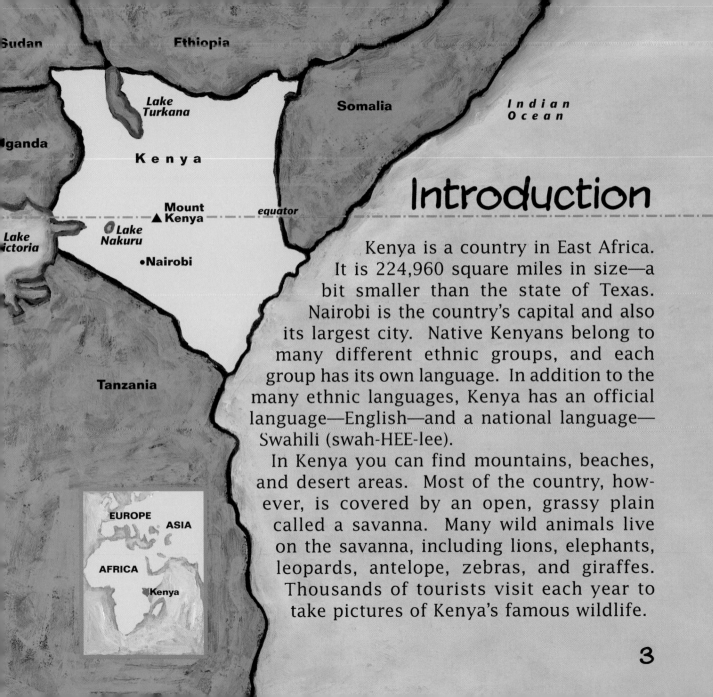

Sudan

Ethiopia

Uganda

Lake
Turkana

Kenya

Somalia

*Indian
Ocean*

Mount
Kenya

equator

Lake
Victoria

Lake
Nakuru

•Nairobi

Tanzania

EUROPE

ASIA

AFRICA

Kenya

Introduction

Kenya is a country in East Africa. It is 224,960 square miles in size—a bit smaller than the state of Texas. Nairobi is the country's capital and also its largest city. Native Kenyans belong to many different ethnic groups, and each group has its own language. In addition to the many ethnic languages, Kenya has an official language—English—and a national language—Swahili (swah-HEE-lee).

In Kenya you can find mountains, beaches, and desert areas. Most of the country, however, is covered by an open, grassy plain called a savanna. Many wild animals live on the savanna, including lions, elephants, leopards, antelope, zebras, and giraffes. Thousands of tourists visit each year to take pictures of Kenya's famous wildlife.

3

4

BLACK

Nyeusi (nyeh-OO-see)

Black is the color of the top stripe on Kenya's flag. The black stripe stands for the people of Kenya. Most of them are black Africans. The native people of Kenya belong to many different ethnic groups. Each ethnic group has its own special language, clothing, and ceremonies. Most Kenyans live in the country or in small villages. They do their shopping at outdoor markets. Some of these Kenyans are farmers or cattle herders. Others are artists who make carvings from wood or stone. Their children play games instead of watching television, because their homes do not have electricity.

Kenyans who live in cities have a different way of life from those who live in the country. Most city people's homes have electricity, and the people shop in stores instead of outdoor markets. They work in factories and other businesses. But whether native Kenyans live in the city or the country, they share at least one thing. They are proud to be black Africans. They are proud of their country—Kenya.

BROWN

Kahawa (kah-HAH-wah)

Most of the houses outside the major Kenyan cities are all the same color—**brown.** Even the roofs are brown. A Kenyan's house might be round or square or shaped like a loaf of bread. Some houses in the highlands and on the savanna have mud walls and roofs made of thatch—dried grass or palm leaves. Other houses are made entirely of pole frames covered with thatch. In the desert areas of the north, grass and leaves are scarce. Here, the houses are made of pole frames covered with sheets of leather.

RED

Nyekundu (Nyeh-KOON-doo)

The Masai (mah-SYE) are one of the ethnic groups that live in Kenya. When you think of the Masai people, think **red**. The traditional cloaks worn by Masai men are red. The men also use red-colored earth called *ochre* (OH-ker) to dye their hair. They wear their long hair styled in many thin braids. Masai women shave their hair off and use the red earth to stain their heads.

Long ago, the Masai men were fierce warriors. Over time, they became cattle herders. A family with many cattle is considered rich. Girls milk the cows. Boys learn from their fathers how to move the cattle from place to place to find food and water. Masai people know each animal in their herd and can tell if one is missing just by looking. You might count the cattle to know if any are missing, but a Masai would not. Counting cattle is thought to be unlucky.

GRAY

Kijivu (kih-JEE-voo)

According to a Kenyan legend, when trees were first planted on Earth, the huge, **gray** baobab (BAY-a-bab) tree refused to stay in one place. Instead, it pulled up its roots and wandered about. Finally, God grew tired of having to replant the tree. To stop the baobab from walking around, God planted the tree upside down.

This is one story that is told to explain the unusual appearance of the baobab tree. All of its branches stick out from the top of the trunk, and it has no leaves for much of the year. It really *does* look root-side up!

During Kenya's dry season, the baobab is a source of water to animals living on the savanna. The tree is soft inside, not hard. This soft wood stores water that the tree soaks up from the ground. When the weather is hot and water is hard to find, elephants rip open the baobab's trunk with their tusks to get at the soggy wood inside. If a baobab is not disturbed, it may live to be two thousand years old!

11

YELLOW

Manjano (mahn-JAHN-oh)

In Kenya, corn is used to make a food called *ugali* (oo-GAH-lee), or *posho* (PO-sho). The corn—**yellow** or white in color—is ground up and mixed with water. This mixture is boiled until it becomes thick and stiff. Everyone makes sure that their hands are clean before eating ugali because—guess what? Ugali is scooped up with fingers, not spoons or forks. At breakfast, ugali is eaten instead of cereal. At dinner, ugali might be served with stew. Then the ugali becomes a spoon. A pot of stew and a big bowl of ugali are set on the table. Each person uses one hand to reach into the bowl of ugali, scoop out some of the mash, and shape it into a small ball. The thumb makes a dent in the ball, giving it a scoop shape. This ugali "spoon" is used to dip out some of the stew. Then the stew and spoon are eaten together.

PINK

Waridi (wah-REE-dee)

Seen from the air, Kenya's blue-green Lake Nakuru appears to have a **pink** ruffle around it. Up close, you can see that the pink ruffle is really hundreds of flamingos wading at the water's edge. They are there to eat the tiny, blue-green algae plants that grow in the lake. This special food gives the flamingo its pink coloring. Lake Nakuru is famous for the flocks of flamingos that gather there. At times, more than a million flamingos are eating, bathing, and marching up and down the shallow lake together. It almost seems as if there are more birds than water! Sometimes a huge flock of flamingos will take off from the lake all at once. The birds look like a big pink cloud in the sky—and sound like a rainstorm. All those wings beating together rumble like thunder across Kenya.

16

GREEN

Kijani kibichi
(Kih-JAHN-ee kih-BEE-chee)

If you were flying over Kenya and saw large **green** areas down below, you would probably be looking at coffee or tea plantations. Coffee and tea are important to Kenya. These crops are grown to sell to other countries.

Perhaps you have seen coffee beans at home or in a store. Coffee beans look very different growing on the plant. In fact, you can't see the beans—they are hidden in the coffee berry. The berry starts out green. As the berry ripens, it turns yellow, then red. Workers walk along neat rows of coffee plants looking for these red, ripe berries. They pick them carefully by hand. Inside each berry are two brown seeds—the coffee beans. A machine separates the beans from the berries, then the beans are spread on racks in the sun to dry.

On tea plantations, the green leaves of tea plants are harvested. Tea leaves, like coffee berries, are picked by hand. Workers put the leaves in large baskets that they wear on their backs.

WHITE

Nyeupe (nyeh-OO-pay)

The top of Mount Kenya is **white** with snow all year. For this reason, the original native name for the mountain was Mountain of Whiteness. When explorers from Europe first saw the mountain, they were surprised by its snow-covered top. Mount Kenya is on the equator. The equator is halfway between the north and south poles and is the hottest area on Earth. The explorers did not expect to find snow at the equator.

At the bottom of Mount Kenya, it is hot all year—just as the European explorers thought it would be. But Mount Kenya is very tall. It is the tallest mountain in Kenya and the second tallest in all of Africa. Clouds often swirl around Mount Kenya's peaks, hiding them from view. The air at the top of Mount Kenya is always cold. When snow falls there, it never melts. Tourists like hiking up Mount Kenya to have snowball fights at the equator!

19

GOLD

Dhahabu (thah-HAH-boo)

Kenyan athletes have won **gold** medals all over the world for long-distance running. The runners get a lot of practice at home. Most people in Kenya do not own cars. They walk to get from place to place. Children may have to walk—or run—a long way to get to school. Kenya's first world record holder for long-distance running was Kipchoge Keino (KIP-chohg KEE-no). He won a gold medal at the 1968 Olympic Games and another one at the 1972 Olympic Games. Kip, as he is often called, also won gold medals at other competitions.

Do you know how your name was chosen? In Kenya, some children are named for what is happening when they are born. Kipchoge Keino was named in this way. *Kip* means "boy," and *choge* means "hour of the day they bring the goats in." So his name says that he is a boy who was born when the goats were being brought in from the pasture.

BLUE

Samawati (sahm-ah-WAH-tee)

What is **blue** and wet and the home of lions that have no legs? The Indian Ocean! This ocean borders Kenya on the east, where white sand beaches sparkle in the sun. In the water is a coral reef. Put on a snorkeling mask and fins and paddle out to the reef. Do you see the lions without legs? They are not the animal called *simba* in Swahili—the lion with fur and a tail. These lions have large, featherlike fins and golden brown stripes. They are lion-fish. Be careful! Lionfish have poisonous spines on their back that can be as dangerous as simba's claws and teeth.

Of course, you will see more than just lionfish at the reef. You will see fish of all shapes and sizes and colors. You would need the biggest box of crayons you could find to draw a picture of these fancy fish!

23

Index